# Reading Together

# OVER IN THE
# MEADOW

*A Counting Rhyme*

# Read it together

*Over in the Meadow* is a picture book version of a traditional counting song. It offers strong support to young readers through rhyme, rhythm, repetition and pictures.

With its growing number of noisy animals this book can be great fun to read aloud – and sing together.

Can we have this book again?

Encourage your child to join in whenever they can, by singing along, by taking over parts of the song themselves, or by talking about the story and pictures.

By hearing the book read aloud again and again, children will get to know the song almost word for word. Don't worry if they say it in their own way.

In the meadow lived a turtle and her baby turtles...

Old MacDonald had some ducks, too. These can be his ducks.

You can use the rhymes and pictures to help your child to guess an unknown word. Encourage children to use their own experiences to make a guess.

*"We buzz," said the Five.* Where do they buzz?

**Round their snug beehive.**

It helps children as readers and writers if they are interested in the look and shape of words and letters. See if they can find words they recognize, letters from their name or even words that are short and long.

**Now we need an "F" for Freddie.**

**We read another book with numbers in it.**

**Yes, that was *Ten in the Bed!***

Children may well enjoy remembering other counting books or songs they know.

We hope you enjoy reading this book together.

*For Gran
Margaret Craig
McDougall*

First published 1994 by Walker Books Ltd
87 Vauxhall Walk, London SE11 5HJ

This edition published 1998

4 6 8 10 9 7 5

Illustrations © 1994 Louise Voce
Introductory and concluding notes © 1998 CLPE/LB Southwark

Printed in Great Britain

ISBN 0-7445-4899-3

# OVER IN THE MEADOW

*A Counting Rhyme*

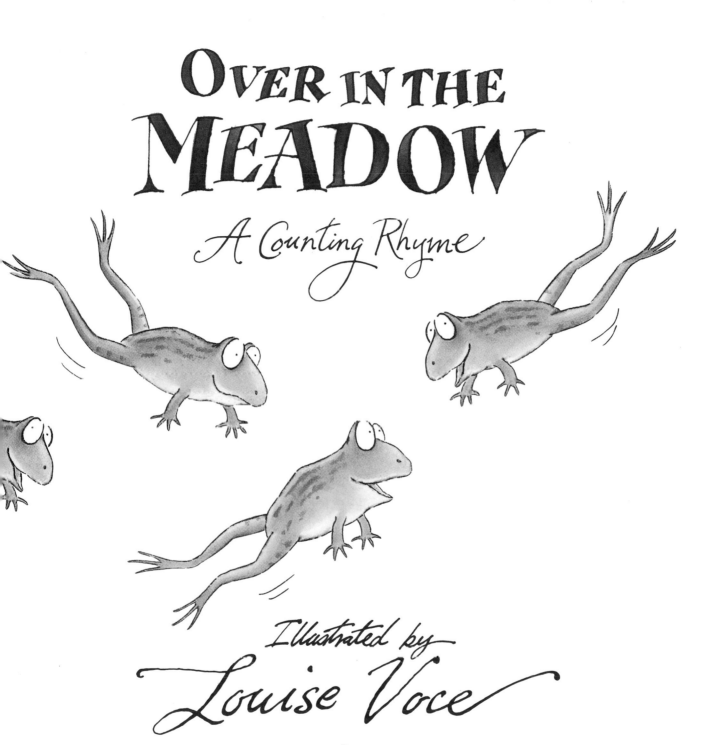

*Illustrated by*
*Louise Voce*

WALKER BOOKS
AND SUBSIDIARIES
LONDON • BOSTON • SYDNEY

# Over
in the meadow
in the sand
in the sun …

Lived an old mother turtle
and her little turtle
# ONE.
"Dig," said his mother.
"I dig," said the One;
So he dug all day
in the sand in the sun.

Over in the meadow
where the stream runs blue,
Lived an old mother duck
and her little ducklings
**TWO.**
"Quack," said their mother.
"We quack," said the Two;
So they quacked all day
where the stream runs blue.

Over in the meadow
in a hole in a tree,
Lived an old mother owl
and her little owls
THREE.
"To-whoo," said their mother.
"To-whoo," said the Three;
So they to-whooed all day
in a hole in a tree.

Over in the meadow
by the big barn door,
Lived an old mother mouse
and her little mice
# FOUR.
"Squeak," said their mother.
"We squeak," said the Four;
So they squeaked all day
by the big barn door.

Over in the meadow
in a snug beehive,
Lived an old mother bee
and her little bees
FIVE.
"Buzz," said their mother.
"We buzz," said the Five;
So they buzzed all day
round their snug beehive.

Over in the meadow
in a nest built of sticks,
Lived an old mother squirrel
and her little squirrels
SIX.
"Jump," said their mother.
"We jump," said the Six;
So they jumped all day
round their nest built of sticks.

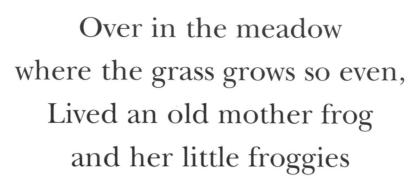

Over in the meadow
where the grass grows so even,
Lived an old mother frog
and her little froggies
SEVEN.
"Hop!" said their mother.
"We hop!" said the Seven;
So they hopped all day
where the grass grows so even.

Over in the meadow
near the little mossy gate,
Lived an old mother lizard
and her little lizards
EIGHT.
"Run," said their mother.
"We run," said the Eight;
So they ran all day
on the little mossy gate.

Over in the meadow
by the tall Scots pine,
Lived an old mother pig
and her little piglets
NINE.
"Oink!" said their mother.
"We oink," said the Nine;
So they oinked all day
near the tall Scots pine.

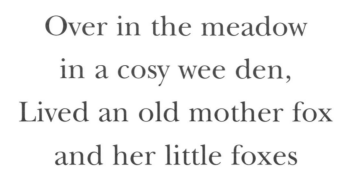

Over in the meadow
in a cosy wee den,
Lived an old mother fox
and her little foxes
TEN.
"Play," said their mother.
"We play," said the Ten;
So they played all day
round their cosy wee den.

Over in the meadow
in the sand in the sun...

1 digs

2 quack

3 to-whoo

4 squeak

5 buzz

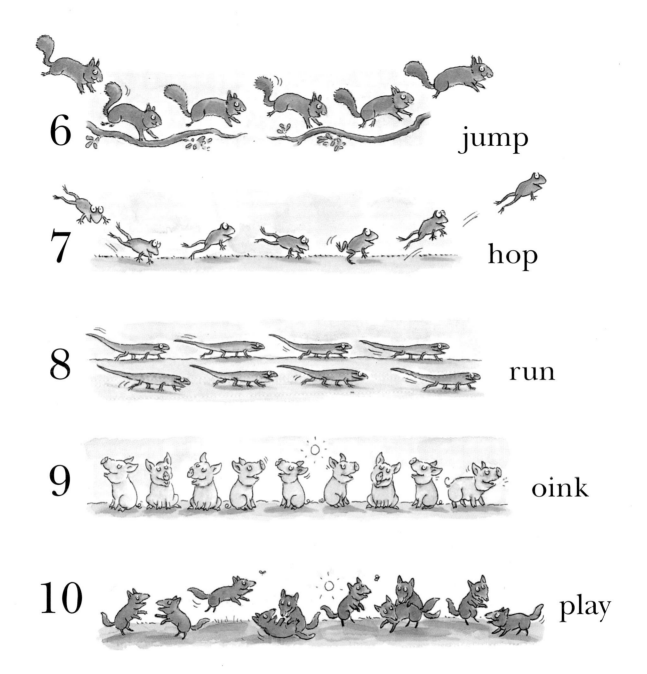

6       jump

7       hop

8       run

9       oink

10      play

over in the meadow
till the end of the day.

# Read it again

## Count the animals

As you read this counting rhyme, your child can join in by finding the animals and counting the babies with their fingers. Children could act out the rhyme, making the animal movements or sounds.

One ... two baby ducklings... Quack! Quack!

## Who lives here?

You can use this picture-map of the story to match the animals to the places where they live: the barn, the beehive, a hole in a tree... Children can search through the book to remind themselves where the animals live. They can also use the picture-map to retell the rhyme or make up stories together about some of the characters in the book.

barn door

gate

grass

beehive

stream

How do I get home?

I'm buzzing back!

Scots pine

den

nest

hole

sand

## Make a counting book

Your child might enjoy making their own counting book. With your help, they can draw or cut out pictures of familiar objects and put them in 1, 2, 3 or 10, 9, 8 order. You could show them different examples by reading other counting rhymes and books.

## Match the numbers

Use the previous two pages to play a matching game. You can make a set of cards with the numbers on and help your child to match them with the pictures.

Can you find where I live?

# Reading Together

The *Reading Together* series is divided into four levels – starting with red, then on to yellow, blue and finally green. The six books in each level offer children varied experiences of reading. There are stories, poems, rhymes and songs, traditional tales and information books to choose from.

Accompanying the series is a Parents' Handbook, which looks at all the different ways children learn to read and explains how *your* help can really make a difference!